Betrayed: A Survivor's Story

By Maraisha Harris-Jackson

The knives of betrayal and drama cut deep and hurt... but they also trim away the nonsense and reveal your true friends.

Betrayal: A Survivor's Story

By Maraisha Harris-Jackson

Dedication

Sitting down and writing all of this has been an incredible experience, and, yes, just in case you're wondering, it's a true story.

I say that here because as you begin reading through all of this, you'll be scratching your head, thinking to yourself, "Oh, COME ON... could this have REALLY happened? Are the police and federal agents and city officials and state-run organizations that corrupt? Does racism like this really STILL exist in this day and age?"

My answer, as you'll discover while reading through, is yes... to all of the above. I have better things to do with my time than to make stuff up and put it into a book, especially one that's labeled "A True Story" right after the title.

These things happened to me, and as I sit here in early March of 2022, I'm 16 years old, going on 17 in two months, and what happened to me starting from the age of seven I wouldn't wish on my worst enemy. I've dealt with the worst of mankind, but also the best, and you sort of forget sometimes that there really are some good people out there. And after you read this, you'll probably think that the bad people in Wilmington, Delaware, outnumber the good people that call this city home.

I still wonder that myself sometimes.

But as my teacher's mother once told him, "That which doesn't kill you, only makes you stronger." And that sure is the case with me and what's happened to me during these past nine years. It's affected not only me, but my grandma and my aunt, the two people in this world that I love more than anything. They've been by my side through thick and thin, and always will be. That's almost more tragic than what happened to me, because they, too, were undeserving victims in all of these little vignettes that you're about to read.

I want to dedicate this book to those from whom I draw my strength. My grandmother (my father's mom), Charmaine Harris; my aunt (grandma's daughter), Aisha Harris; my "spiritual" mother and father from the church, Sherfone Williams and Joseph Williams; my dad's nephew, Raheem Harris; and my online reading teacher, Eric Hanson, who helped me put all of these feelings onto paper.

I hope that my story inspires those who might have been abused or are STILL being abused to talk with someone about it, your grandma, aunt, mom or dad, a friend... ANYBODY. Just let somebody know. Don't let the abusers have the chance to abuse again, and I hope that if you're a past victim of mental or physical abuse (or both) that you'll draw some strength from all this.

God knows that I have.

Many such victims spend their entire lives keeping their secrets of abuse to themselves, and those repressed feelings sometimes come out in the form of bad actions, sadness and/or anger and, worse of all, aggressive behavior. Many such people who are abused as children become abusers themselves with THEIR children, and the ugly cycle repeats itself.

It's not a fun read, but it's true... take from it what you will.

At the beginning of the Walt Disney book "Cinderella," Cinderella's mother is lying on her deathbed, and she made Cinderella say the following promise:

"Be courageous and kind, for kindness has power and magic."

By that, her mother meant that having these special traits would see Ella through all the trials and tribulations that life would offer.

And I sure found at a young age that if there's one thing that life is sure full of, it's trials.

I hope you like my story.

CHAPTER ONE: Kindergarten

It all started when I was in kindergarten. I was a kind, sweet, loving girl (and I still consider myself to be much the same). I loved school and went there happily every day.

Past tense. Not anymore. In fact, the only type of schooling that I truly enjoy and get anything out of is my online tutoring. THAT is enjoyable; THAT I learn from. But going to a brick-and-mortar school? Nope. There is absolutely no enjoyment in that.

It all began one day when I was goofing around with my friends, acting like a child (which is exactly what I was, seeing how I was in kindergarten at this time),

Joseph and Sherfone Williams, my spritual parents.

laughing, not paying attention... you know; typical kid stuff.

Suddenly, a teacher *(I'll call her Mrs. Johnson)* got frustrated with me and forced me to sit down; then, suddenly, out of nowhere, she slapped me fast and hard across my face... in full view of the entire class. Nothing like that to emotionally scar a child, wouldn't you agree?

Now, naturally, as a kid, I'm thinking to myself at the time, why would a teacher that is supposed to educate, love, protect and encourage kids suddenly, out of nowhere, hit me, just because we were acting up and perhaps being a bit too noisy? Being as young as I was, I wasn't sure if this was typical behavior for a teacher to exhibit towards her students... but I was pretty sure that it wasn't.

I was hurt, both physically and emotionally, and worse yet, I felt humiliated and ashamed. Now, the other kids in class weren't laughing at me, and that's a good thing in terms of my self-esteem. No, they were sitting there with looks of shock on their faces, and I could tell that they were thinking, *'OH GOD, PLEASE DON'T LET ME BE THE NEXT ONE!'*

And then, to make a horrible situation even worse, Mrs. Johnson grabbed me with both hands on my shoulders and slammed me into my chair, which was against a wall. My whole body rammed against that wall, and judging by how hard I hit it, I could tell that she was MORE than just plain old angry. But... for something like THIS? I'd hate to see how she'd handle a REAL problem in class!

I felt a horrific pain in my back and my right arm, and at this point, that pain was beginning to radiate throughout my entire body.

Coincidentally, at that very moment, I heard my name being announced over the school intercom, asking me to please come down to the front office. Now, I had already had a doctor's appointment lined up for that same day to get a school physical exam, and I had to assume that my being called to the office was because my grandmother was there waiting to pick me up.

Mrs. Johnson then roughly grabbed me by my right arm, yanked me out of my chair and proceeded to practically drag me down the hall to meet my grandmother. And all the while, I was wondering to myself, 'What is grandma gonna think when she sees my teacher dragging me in like a bag of potatoes?'

I was too young to realize that what was going on was beyond unacceptable; I thought that I must have brought this on myself.

When the two of us arrived at the office and walked in the front door, Mrs. Johnson's demeanor did a complete 180. She suddenly became a sweet-faced, concerned, happy teacher, who radiated a not-a-care-in-the-world persona which was in stark contrast of what she had transformed into not 10 minutes prior. I couldn't believe what I was seeing; this of course HAD to be some sort of demented nightmare... NONE of this could really be happening!

"Don't forget your homework," Mrs. Johnson said with a sticky-sweet, fake voice as she jammed the papers into my hand. Because of where we were standing in the office, my grandmother and the principal didn't see this rough behavior.

As my grandmother and I walked out of the office, I kept hearing from behind, "Bye, have a nice day! Bye! Bye!"

This was the very definition of surreal. My grandmother and I got into her car and began the drive to my doctor's appointment. I felt a wave of guilt, shock, fear, confusion, bewilderment and sadness overcome me, and instead of telling my grandmother what had just happened, I sat there in silence until we got to the doctor's office. I realized later that I should have immediately said something, but I was a kid who, during the past 10 minutes, had just met the devil incarnate, and I was just too scared to speak up.

We arrived to the doc's office a few minutes later and sat in the waiting room. A short time later, she called me in and had me sit on the typical cold, aluminum exam table covered with that insanely thin layer of tissue (we all know that table very well). She began looking me over, here and there, up and down, poking here, inspecting there, when suddenly she stopped after noticing my back.

"What happened here?" she said suddenly and with obvious shock. There, on my back, neck and right arm was a long, black-and-blue bruise that ran from my neck, over the rear of my arm and down my back.

My grandmother looked equally surprised and appalled.

"What happened?" grandma gasped with a mixture of anger and shock.

I put my head down, teared up and told my grandmother and the doctor the entire story, from the moment I walked into class up until Mrs. Johnson dragged me down to the office and met my grandmother with that stupid, fake smile of hers.

Now, my grandma had always told me to tell her right away if anything bad ever happened to me, and I thought that I would be in big trouble because I didn't tell her when we got into the car at school.

Grandma looked at me. "You should have told me at the school that the teacher put her hands on you!" she said, but not in an angry way... more out of disbelief.

My doctor proceeded with the physical and then put my story into my medical records. After grandma and I got home, she immediately called the school and told them what had happened. The next day, she went down, met with the school principal and gave him the run-down. She then showed him the pictures that she had taken of me on her cell phone at the doctor's office.

Grandma said that the principal sat there with his mouth open as he looked at the damage that had been done to my body and told grandma that he would take care of this "immediately, if not sooner."

My grandmother wanted to make sure that this would be more than just a case of a little girl's word against a teacher's, so she marched down to Mrs. Johnson's office and said that she wanted her to immediately have the school's security tapes pulled and given to her, right then and there.

The principal immediately retrieved the tapes and watched them with grandma and a few other school officials.

After the viewing, the principal picked up his phone and called Delaware Family Services, a state-run organization that helps families in situations such as this, and made an over-the-phone report. After hanging up with them, he called the state's licensing board and, in turn, told them what had happened. The board immediately revoked Mrs. Johnson's teaching license and the principal naturally fired her.

This was the first of many such betrayals. And lest you forget... this one happened in kindergarten.

Things weren't so bad for the next few years... until I reached fifth grade. And that's where the horror show once again reared its ugly head.

CHAPTER TWO: Fifth Grade

Getting over the kindergarten episode was still something that I was wrestling with, and as a result, I was carrying around a lot of aggression, anger and emotional pain. In other words, I wasn't a joy to be around. Not by a long shot.

So, fifth grade kicks into gear; up until this point, I had spent the previous four grades at school with an assortment of racists of every skin color: white, light-skinned black children and other kids who were of a different skin shade than myself, either darker or lighter or somewhere in between.

One thing that this world is in no short supply of is... racists.

And with every new grade and with every new batch of racist tauntings, I could not figure out one very important thing: why were other kids who were black like me PICKING on me? This made no sense at all. The way I saw it, and still do, is that we're

My mother

ALL BLACK, we're all in the same boat together, so why in the world were these boys and girls saying such horrible racist things towards a fellow black child? It made no sense whatsoever; still doesn't.

Now, my online teacher once told me that kids are inherently mean, no matter what their color and no matter what color they're picking on. They say and do horrible things to each other, but this sort of abuse was a real head-scratcher.

I'd been doing gymnastics since the age of two, and I was enrolled in the elementary P.E. program. As a result of hundreds of hours spent working out and eating only what was good for me, it was paying off: my body was getting toned and muscular... not too much so as to look bulked up like a guy, but I was in great shape, better shape than most fifth-graders.

This found me in the cross-hairs of other students who poked fun at me merely because I was in shape and took care of myself. And this was something ELSE that I couldn't understand... normally, other mean kids pick on and tease the overweight kids, NOT the kids who are... in shape and take care of themselves. Strange.

The racist slurs and the bullies and their horrible insults followed me from grade to grade, year to year, and every time that I entered a new grade, I prayed to God that I would find a new group of friends who saw me as I was and that the bullies would just disappear.

But I guess that God was too busy to hear me.

****

A little bit about me.

I have three brothers and two sisters: four come from my mom's side, including me, my older brother, my older sister and my little brother. The other two are from my dad's previous marriage: a little brother and another little sister.

Mom and dad never tied the knot, and my older brother and I have always been closer than close. I have no relationship in any way, shape, manner or form with the kids on my mom's side, but I'm really close with my dad's son and daughter. We talk a lot, and that's a beautiful thing.

I've lived with my grandmother since I was a baby. My natural father, who was a huge part of my life, passed away four years ago when I was 12. We were two peas in a pod, and he was my "go-to" person in all things important. I miss him and think of him every day, but... the conversation continues (my grandma, by the way,was dad's mother, just for reference).

My mother was (and is) a different story, and not in a good way, either. She kicked my dad and I out of the house when I was just a baby, and not because he wasn't earning money for the family. He made sure that we had a roof over our heads and food on the table, and to this day I still don't know why she did it.

And apparently, I never will.

The worse part is, she tells me that she still doesn't know why she gave us the boot. Before she even met my father, she was diagnosed with schizophrenia as well as Bi-Polar 1 and Bi-Polar 2 (a clinical definition of this disease is as follows: *"Manic episodes may include symptoms such as high energy, reduced need for sleep, and loss of touch with reality. Depressive episodes may include symptoms such as low energy, low motivation, and loss of interest in daily activities. Mood episodes last days to months at a time and may also be associated with suicidal thoughts.")*

My mother decided to come back into my life here and there after dad's passing, but she does it more or less when it's convenient for her. She's a constant no-show for holidays, and naturally, we just don't talk that much... sometimes for months at a time. It's just who she is, and for better or for worse, I've grown accustomed to it.

I asked her a while back why she kicked dad and I out of the house so many years ago, especially in light of the fact that I was just a baby at the time.

"It just wasn't a good fit," she told me. To this day, I still don't understand what that means. Friends might not be a good fit together; even couples who have been dating for a short period of time go through this on occasion and decide to call it quits. But a mother... telling her daughter... that she wasn't "a good fit"? Incomprehensible, even as I sit here, putting ink to paper.

July 4th, 2018. I'm 12 years old at this time and dad had passed away in April of this same year. I was living with grandma, and on this particular day, she decided to invite mom over to the house to celebrate the nation's birthday. Try to have some fun, maybe even bond a bit... stuff like that.

So much for good intentions on my part.

My precious dad,Marshall Harris

Before I went to mom's house, grandma and I had what we call a 'balloon release' at her house to mark my dad's passing. I tied a picture of grandma and I to the small helium balloon and released it into the air. It was just our beautiful way of saying that we hoped he'd get the picture... and I know that he did.

Mom had invited only me over to her house for the day. I thought, hey, it might be fun, maybe we could actually talk for once, get to know each other, put the past behind us as best we could.

But, that's not exactly what happened. No, sir. In fact, the complete OPPOSITE happened, and to this day I rue the moment that I accepted that invitation.

When I arrived there, we sat and talked for a while about nothing of any great concern. I was telling mom about a guy that I liked, whom I naturally assumed was about my age, give or take, but we'll get to that later.

My mother had invited this "boy" over to her house *(we'll call him Joe)* which at first sounded like a nice thing to do. He arrived at around 10 that night, walks into the house and sits down. Now, my 18-year-old sister *(we'll call her Sue)* lives with my mother, and she was there when Joe walked into mom's house.

Joe had previously told me that he was 13, but it turns out that my sister KNEW Joe, and he was not 13. Not hardly.

I found this out while my sister and Joe started talking in front of me. She asked him how old he was. His response: "I'm 18 years old." Now, I'm no math wizard, but 18 is five years old than 13. And, as I found out later, there are laws against these kinds of things...

Now, keep in mind that my mother was in the kitchen and heard Joe say that he was 18. She obviously had no problem with that... which to me... is a problem. What kind of a mother condones her barely teenage daughter hooking up with a man of 18?

I was beyond speechless. I turned around, walked upstairs and into the bathroom and mom followed right behind me.

"You're spending the night here because I can't get a ride to bring you back to grandma's," she said. "Go ahead and take a shower, change and come downstairs. Your company is waiting for you." Mom then went into her bedroom.

So I did exactly that and went downstairs a short time later. My sister was playing a video game and Joe was in the kitchen, but came into the living room when he heard me.

I sat on the couch and he sat down next to me, and a few minutes later my sister went upstairs to go and get something out of her room. She came back, continued playing her game for a few minutes, then fell asleep there in the living room on another couch.

 I started to feel a bit uncomfortable around Joe and already had a headache from the smell and sound of the fireworks outside, so I went upstairs to see if my mother had an aspirin. She said that she didn't, but gave me some sort of peach-colored gel tablet which I promptly swallowed.

I went back downstairs and Joe said, "Why didn't you just tell *me* that you had a headache? I've got something for you." He gave me a pill that he promised would "get the headache away quicker." (To this day, I still have no idea what type of pill it was).

I sat back down on the couch and, after a few minutes, I started getting extremely dizzy and my body felt as limp as a newborn baby. I still had my senses about me, but it was such a new, horrendous feeling, one I'll never forget.

To make a long story short, he sexually assaulted me and I was pretty much powerless to stop him. This went off-and-on from late in the evening until early in the morning. There was no sexual intercourse involved, but just about everything else.

I woke up the next morning and was drowning in a whirlpool of emotions: I was embarrassed; I was angry; I felt violated; I felt sad; I was irritated; I felt helpless; I felt... alone. I went downstairs and, to make matters even worse, Joe was still there, sitting on the couch... waiting for me.

My sister walked into the living room and she overheard some of the things that Joe was saying to me, like how much he liked me and wanted to... "get to know me" better.

I sort of know now what that meant then.

My sister, as horrible as she is, is nobody's fool, and she had a pretty good idea of what happened upstairs the night before.

"You're too young to be doing stuff like this," she hissed at me. "You're too young to be using the "F" word."

Obviously, I had no idea what she was talking about since there was no actual

Yours truly

Me, age 15

Me, age 13

My aunt, Aisha Harris

intercourse. Instead of directing her rage at Joe, she turned it at ME, which obviously made no sense at all. *I'm* the little sister, and Sue is my big sister. The last time I checked, the big sister is supposed to take care of the little sister and make sure that things like this don't happen.

But that wasn't the case. Sue LET this happen to me, and to make things even worse, she points the finger of blame at me. And to this day, I still have no idea why. Joe was an 18-year-old aggressor, an ADULT as far as the law is concerned, and I was a 13-year-old kid who didn't know any better. Even if Joe had claimed that he didn't know that it was illegal to do this kind of stuff with a 13-year-old, just the fact that he was 18, he should have known better. He should have known that you don't do this kind of stuff with a kid.

So, I looked back at Sue and lost whatever cool it was that I still had left. I screamed and yelled and cursed her out, throwing things at her in the process.

Mom heard the commotion and ran downstairs; to make a long story short, she sided with Sue, even though she didn't even know what was going on.

My darling mother got in my face, screaming, "You can go back to your grandma's house and get the f**k out of here! You can't talk to MY DAUGHTER like that; I taught her how to kill, and I'll have her kill you if I want to!"

Strange use of vocabulary... she said this as though Sue were her ONLY daughter. The last time I checked, mom had given birth to two daughters, me and Sue. Where did this 'my daughter' singular come from?

Now, as much as I wanted to get out of there as quickly as possible, mom didn't have a way for to get me back to grandma's house, so I was forced to stay another night in that hellhole of a house.

I spent the night listening to music and crying. Joe had left during the aforementioned screaming match, but sleep was the last thing that came to me that night.

****

The next day, mom tried to smooth things over by taking me to McDonald's, but her true intentions were to keep my mouth shut and not to let grandma know what had gone down.

But of course, I told grandma, who was furious to the 1,000th degree and wanted to press criminal charges against my mom and Joe. I talked her out of that, much against her wishes. Today, though, almost four years after this occurred, I really wish that I had let grandma press those charges. And here's a kicker... Joe told me that he'd gotten a 16-year-old girl pregnant.

"How could you let somebody treat you like that and not want to DO something?" grandma asked, exasperated. But I instead made a promise to myself: just keep away from mom's house and avoid her and Sue at all costs.

And to this day, five years later, I've made good on that promise. I haven't seen either one of them since then and don't care if I ever do again.

****

When I was seven, I was diagnosed with ADHD (Attention Deficit Hyperactivity

Disorder). The reasons behind this are many: starting from a young age, I had a lot of internal anger, aggression and a short fuse, all of which got me into a lot of knock-down fights. At this point in my life, if anybody looked at me cross-eyed, I would be on them like white on rice. The police never got involved and during school, I was just put in "time-out" as punishment.

Big deal. Accomplished nothing.

Another reason for the diagnosis is that I was as hyper as can be imagined. At school, I would run around the building as though my pants were on fire, over and over, around and around, just to avoid going to class. Needless to say, I wasn't a big fan of school, and did whatever I could to avoid going into the next period: hiding in the girls' room, telling my teachers that I was sick and had to go to the nurse's office, things like that.

CHAPTER THREE

Well, boys and girls, just when you thought things couldn't get any worse...

When I entered the fourth grade, I had a "para-professional" teacher *(we'll call him Mr. Smith.* His title sounds high-falootin' but it simply means that he was an unlicensed teacher who works in a classroom under the supervision of a licensed teacher (it's part of the process people go through before they become state-licensed instructors). But unfortunately, Mr. Smith never had anybody watching over ***him;*** had that been the

Me, age 4

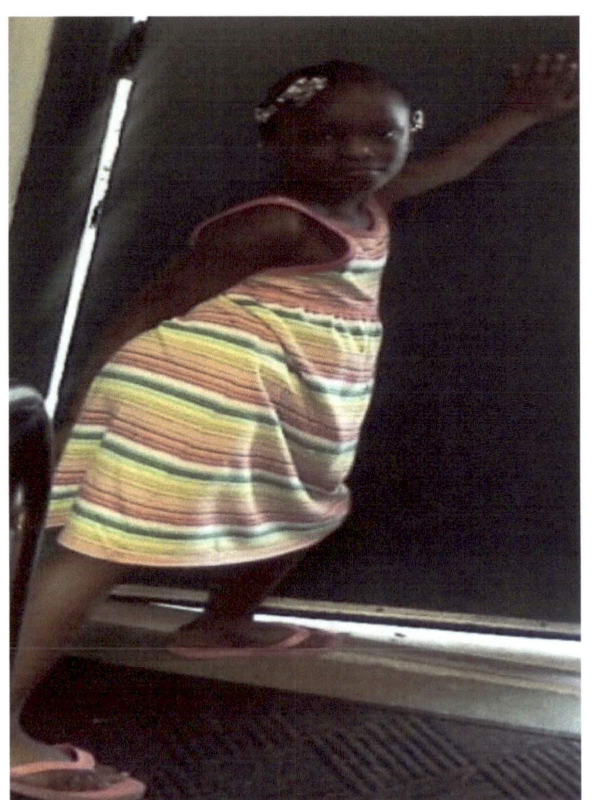

Me, about age

Me, about age 2

Me, age 8

case, this part of my story might never have happened.

This is where the real fun starts, where I found out what 'betrayal' was really all about... first-hand.

Now, Mr. Smith had a bit of an attitude problem, and I'm being totally objective when I say that. One day, the other kids were heading off to lunch and I decided to stay behind and ask him a question about a worksheet that I had to turn in.

He went over everything with me, but due to my diagnosis and the fact that I was a bit slow in processing new information, I asked him to please repeat what he had just gone over.

His gruff response: "I've told you once and I'm not going to repeat myself."

How's that for a quality teacher?

I came back with, "How am I supposed to turn this in if you aren't even going to help me?" To pat myself on the back a bit, most kids would have just said, okay, great, and... left. But I didn't; I wanted to do the assignment correctly, and I needed his help.

His response? "Get out of my fu---ing face."

I looked at him with complete disbelief. "How rude!" I said, almost laughing at how surreal the whole thing was.

Mr. Smith then quickly stood up, and at this age, he looked as tall as The Jolly Green Giant. I stepped back a few steps, but he reached over, grabbed my arm and shoved me with all his might into a brick wall. My back hit first and took the brunt of the impact.

I quickly stood up; Mr. Smith lunged at me, grabbed me by the arm and tossed me right across a table and into the same brick wall. He then jumped at me, slapping, beating and punching me all over my body.

Part of Mr. Smith's licensure requirements was that he to be under constant supervision by another faculty member while he was with students.

Well, here's the problem, folks. This particular fourth grade class started MONTHS before this attack, and not ONCE was there an in-class supervisor watching over Mr. Smith. Not once. Never. Nobody. Smith was going rogue the entire time, which was completely against the rules not only for him becoming licensed, but against school rules, too. And against state regulations as well.

To this day, I wonder if anybody in the office knew about this lack of supervision, and if they did, did they even care. Probably not.

Mr. Smith's beatings and slappings lasted just under five minutes; at this point, I was spread out on the floor. He quickly grabbed my shoulders with both hands, yanked me up and pulled me about an inch from his face, which was contorted and white with rage.

"If you tell anyone, and I mean ANYONE," he whispered at me, staring through my eyes and into my heart, "I... will... *kill.... you.*"

I looked back at him... and believed him. To say that I was merely 'scared' just doesn't cut it... I was petrified to my soul.

He let me go, whirled around and stormed out of the room, slamming the door behind him as he left. The noise that door made sounded like a cannon, and I can still hear it today.

I left the room as well and went to the school auditorium, hanging out there until school was over. I felt hurt, both physically and mentally, embarrassed that I was treated like a bad dog in front of my classmates and, moreover, scared that if I dared breathe a word of this, that it might be my last breath ever.

I took what Mr. Smith said seriously. Any child – or adult, for that matter – would.

Once again, here I was, the victim of a vicious attack by yet another teacher. What were the odds? Maybe I should try playing the lottery when I get older...

I went home; grandma was sitting in a chair in the living room, looking through her mail as she did a million times before on days just like this.

I walked up to her and, still sitting, she gave me a big hug, as she did a million times before on days... just like this.

"Go change out of your school clothes," she said, smiling. But as she hugged me, I flinched because my entire body hurt from the beating. I flinched, and grandma sensed that.

"Are you okay?" she asked, looking at me with grandmotherly concern.

"Yes," I lied.

I then went to my bedroom, changed out of my school clothes and threw them into the washing machine. I didn't tell her what had happened that day because I truly thought that Mr. Smith would kill me and maybe even my grandma.

My cousin, Johnny, who the police
kept looking for while they destroyed our apartments

Me, 2022

And you know something? He probably would have.

I sat down with my grandma at the kitchen table to do some homework, and that's when she saw the day's bruises all over my arms, my thighs, my legs...

"What happened?" she gasped.

"You have to promise me that if I tell you, you won't tell anybody else, because I don't want to die."

My grandmother looked at me with such a look of disbelief.

"What are you talking about?" she demanded.

So I told her.

"Oh my God, that bastard!" she yelled, promising me that when she calmed, she was going down to the school, come hell or high water.

"I'm not ready to die!" I cried.

"You're not going to die," grandma said calmly and reassuringly. "I promise you, you're not going to die."

I believed her.

The next day, grandma lived up to her word and with me in tow, went right down to that school, fit to be tied. She stormed in and verbally tore the heads off of anyone that she came in contact with at that office: the secretary, the janitor, the receptionist, the assistant, anyone within earshot.

The principal *(we'll call him Mr. Jones)* was hiding out in his office behind a closed door and apparently wanted nothing to do with my very angry grandmother. Now, we weren't sure as to whether the principal actually knew what had transpired the day before, but based on the fact that there was yelling and screaming in his outer office and he never even poked his head out to see what was going on, I had to assume that he knew and wanted no part of it.

Yeah... that's a pretty valid assumption.

Grandma and I waited outside his office for about an hour; he never came out. At this point, grandma's anger was in the stratosphere, so she called my father on her cell and told him everything that I told her the day before

My dad was already driving when he took the call, and he apparently made a U-turn and high-tailed it to the school, getting there in minutes. Grandma told me later that all my father heard was "a male teacher put his hands on your daughter." That was enough. It was his little girl. That's all he had to hear.

To get into the school, as is the case with any school these days, you have to push a button outside the main door, look up at the monitor and state your business. Then you're buzzed in or turned away.

When my dad arrived and went through the above-mentioned routine, the principal's office was waiting for him. They apparently saw a very angry father in the monitor and... waited... to buzz him in. They were in no rush for the hellstorm that they knew was coming.

My grandmother looked at the person behind the counter and said, through pursed lips, "You let that man in; that's her father."

The person with his finger on the buzzer looked at my grandmother, looked back at my father's face in the monitor, and then back at my grandmother. I think that he knew that no matter what he did, there would be a boatload of trouble from either my grandmother or my father. So, he begrudgingly pressed the button... and waited.

My father stormed into the office, brushed right through the people working in the front, found the principal's door and began slamming his fists into it.

"Sorry, I can't talk right now," came the principal's voice through the door. "I'm having a meeting."

Needless to say, dad didn't care about any stupid meeting and tried to go inside, but the door was locked (of course it was!). Dad punched the door in frustration and then returned to the outer office and sat down with my grandma and I.

About an hour later, the principal emerged and told us that he was free to talk. (For whatever it's worth, there was nobody else in the office when he came out. Telephone or computer meeting? Maybe. Maybe not.)

But here's the clincher: the principal came out right before the school's dismissal time, and one of his responsibilities was to go outside and watch the students being loaded on the buses. So, as a result, he told my dad that he really didn't have that much time for a sit-down talk.

This was yet more gasoline poured on my dad's fire, and grandma later told me that he was about 10 seconds away from flooring the principal, right there in the office.

Grandma then told dad that it was more than obvious that the principal was blowing us off, so she told him to go to her house so that they could contact the authorities and get this whole thing moving in the right direction.

****

Now Comes the Trauma

The three of us got to grandma's house a short time later, and grandma telephoned the school's resource officer (who is a police detective; we'll call him Detective Mitchell). Now, grandma had previously met the detective after a similar incident with another of her grandchildren.

We told Mitchell the whole horrid story and he assured us that they would initiate pressing charges against the teacher and that he "would pay dearly" for what he did to me.

A week or two passed and we heard nothing from the detective, so we called him at his office. No answer. We tried the same thing daily about five more times; nothing. This went on for about eight days, give or take. Each time, we left a voicemail to have him please return our call. After not having any of our calls returned, we called the district school board.

They gave us the same song and dance: we'll call you if you have any information. And, you guessed it, nobody called.About a month later, our phone had not rung once so then we called the state's child protective services division and told them the whole story. And here's the incredible response from their end: sorry, but we can't help you.

My mother's daughter "Sue"

Nya, my sister from my dad's side

Grandma

Eric Hanson, my online teacher

That's because the assault was NOT started by a family member but by... a teacher. And for some reason, this was, in their own warped vision, okay.

They told us to... call the police. We told child protective that we had already done that, unsuccessfully, and THAT'S WHY we were contacting them.

Sorry... can't help you. "Unless it's a family member physically putting their hands on you, there's just nothing we can do," the woman said.

Back at square one.

And to this day, the good detective has not returned one phone call. There's been absolutely no communication of any kind with him or anyone else in the Wilmington Police Department. Mr. Smith hasn't been questioned by any legal authorities and, of course, has not been arrested. Nothing has been done, and I'll bet you dollars to donuts that nothing ever WILL be done about this.

 Later that school year, I overheard Detective Mitchell in school warning some of the school staff administrators in the school office to permanently shut down the surveillance cameras in my classroom. What if people ask questions, somebody asked? Just tell them that the cameras aren't working.

Yep. You read that right.

And here's the kicker: Detective Mitchell had no idea that I overheard him saying this. I just happened to be walking past the office when it occurred.

Kicker number two: Mr. Smith was still a teacher at my school. That's right. And guess who had him for one of her upcoming classes? Guessed right again.

I'll never forget walking back into his classroom the first day after all of the aforementioned went down. It was more than obvious that he knew that I had contacted the principal and the police and the state's child protective services. As I mentioned a few paragraphs back, he hadn't been arrested, but he knew... everything that my family had done and everybody that we had contacted.

I could see it in his face.

From Betrayal... To Trauma

So, just when you think things can't get much worse... guess what?

Jump ahead to fourth grade. I'm at the ripe old age of 7, attending a charter school straight out of the Middle Ages. I'm still getting bullied about the same stupid things: the tone of my skin, my body being in such good shape, the same-old, same-old.

The girls would insult me and call me 'ugly' to my face. When you're seven, you believe those horrible things. Kids are mean... always have been, always will be. They insulted the clothes that I wore to school, even though I was dressed like any other seven-year-old girl. So, pretty much everything that was me, was insulted. Five days a week; relentlessly. Like clockwork.

The wonderful girls of this school *(we'll call it The School of Misery)* were nothing more than a bunch of back-stabbing, lying fakers who tried jumping me each and every day, just looking for a fight. I always fought back, and I'm proud that I did. There wasn't a lot of actual physical fighting because they knew they were dealing with a cornered tiger. But it still made my days there hell.

Out of all the teachers that I dealt with on a daily basis, there was one that I thought I could trust... emphasis on the word "thought." Now, I didn't tell her anything that had happened before in this book, but I was just looking for a friend. I was lost and looking for a helping hand, and it SEEMED as though an adult teacher would fit this bill, because at this point, my life was not getting any better, and it seemed as though my entire world was crashing down on me. Aside from grandma, my dad and my aunt, I couldn't trust anybody else.

All my life, I've had it hard, and if you've come this far in the book, you can see that this is no lie. But you know something? One of my teachers once told me, "That which doesn't kill you, only makes you stronger." And that's really been the case with me. I'm a strong, confident, beautiful young woman who's had her share of back-stabbing "friends" who smiled in my face while they dug the dagger in as deeply as they could in my back.

This same teacher told me that I'll more than likely encounter these types of people as I go through life, that it's not something that just 'goes away' as I get older. That's why I'm learning that it takes time to fully trust people, and, as I'm finding out, some people are worth the wait.

****

Trauma

February 8th, 2014.

I was home with my aunt because my uncle was in the hospital on his deathbed, and I was obviously too young to be there to see such a heartbreaking event go down.

My dad was there, too, cutting one of his friend's hair when all of a sudden about six police cars pulled into the driveway. We didn't see them arrive, and that's exactly what they were hoping for.

A small handful of cops then snuck up the outside stairs of my aunt's apartment complex, went to her front door and knocked. My dad's friend opened the door and the cops suddenly barged their way in, guns drawn, screaming, *"ON THE FLOOR! ON THE FLOOR! ON THE FLOOR!"*

I was sitting on the couch and just... froze.

About four cops, still with pistols in hand, ran to me on the couch.

"PUT YOUR HANDS UP!" one of them screamed at me, as though he'd just found Al Capone. I of course put them up as quickly as possible.

"What's your name?" one of them snarled at me.

Being seven years old and beyond petrified at this moment, I did what any seven-year-old would do in such a situation: I lied my butt off and told them that my name was Rachel Harmony.

And the best part was... they believed me.

"Why aren't you at school?" he asked, which in all reality was a valid question because it was around 8:00 in the morning, and here I was, not in school.

I told the officer that I was given a personal grievance day to deal with my dying uncle.

My aunt finally spoke up and demanded to know what they were doing and who they were looking for; turns out, they were looking for aunt's son *(we'll call him Jimmy)*. My aunt said that he wasn't there and then asked what they needed with Jimmy. They told my aunt that they received an anonymous call stating that he had stolen a cellphone.

My aunt and the rest of us thought that storming through the door like that with pistols drawn was just a BIT too over-the-top for a person who they *thought* had stolen a phone. So, after answering a few questions from Wilmington's finest, they left.

I should point out that at NO TIME during this entire event did ANY of those cops produce a search warrant, which, as anyone who's ever watched a TV crime show knows, you must produce to the person who answers the door BEFORE you can storm your way in. Doesn't matter if you're looking for Adolf Hitler: a warrant is a warrant, and it must be produced. Period. It's been that way for a long time now.

Now, they do have what are known as "No-Knock" warrants, which mean the police have the right to either open your unlocked door or to pick it open without the benefit of a knock. But this was not such a warrant.

My aunt then phoned my grandma and gave her the run-down about what happened.

"Those bastards," grandma replied under her breath.

Now, the very next day, a repeat performance of what happened at my aunt's house happened... at my grandmother's house; once again, six squad cars come ripping into the front of her apartment complex, six police officers come running up the stairs to her second-floor apartment (I should point out that grandma and my aunt both live in the same building, different floors).

They knocked; my aunt happened to be at grandma's house and answered the door. THIS time, my aunt invited them in; they apparently didn't feel it necessary to barge their way in.

Now, my aunt let the cops in intentionally, knowing that it would rile grandma... and it worked.

Grandma ran up to the officers and began to shake her cane at them. If one of them tried to enter, say, a bedroom, grandma stuck out her cane in front of them and blocked their entry. The officers said that they had received yet another anonymous phone call that Jimmy had stolen another phone, which we knew to be not true.

This went on for a few minutes, and the officers (who called grandma 'crazy lady') decided to leave and avoid any further confrontation.

"Don't you EVER let those bastards come into my house again!" grandma yelled at my aunt.

Easier said than done.

****

January 18th, 2022. And the beat goes on.

A little after 5:30 in the morning, the police came again and THIS TIME broke down grandma's front door with a battering ram, without even the benefit of a knock.

Needless to say, the three of us were fast asleep and had no idea what was going on.

My aunt was sleeping in the living room, so naturally they approached her first, guns drawn once again.

"LAY DOWN! LAY DOWN!" they screamed. (Since my aunt was already laying down in the FIRST PLACE, this... didn't really make a lot of sense. But I digress...)

My aunt naturally began to scream; I was sleeping with my grandma in her master bedroom and I woke up, not knowing what the hell was going on.

The police began searching the apartment and finally made their way into grandma's room. Her door was locked and I heard from the other side, "THIS DOOR IS LOCKED! You'd better open this f****ing door before I f***ing shoot it open!"

Now, my sister *(on my father's side; we'll call her Nya)* was also in grandma's bedroom and woke up only after I started screaming, "DON'T SHOOT ME! DON'T SHOOT ME!" At this point, Nya dashes into grandma's bathroom, trying her best to hide.

I quickly unlocked the door and jumped back from it, not knowing what to expect when it opened. A total of 13 – that's right, 13 – officers bolted into the room, guns drawn.

Now, here's the most amazing thing of all. Outside the door there were about 20 – yes, 20 – FBI agents and about a dozen state troopers, not including the 13 Wilmington Police Department officers. The FBI agents and the local police waited outside the door, and it was the state troopers that made their way into grandma's house. It looked to me as though every law enforcement officer in Delaware was there.

Anyway, I laid down on the ground, as motionless as possible. One thing I remember vividly is that as our eyes met, I could tell that they would shoot me, no questions asked, and not even blink.

They screamed at grandma to put up her hands, which she tried to do but in light of the fact that she has arthritis, it wasn't an easy thing to do.

One of the officers ran into the bathroom and saw Nya trying to hide and screamed at her, *"GET OUT OF THERE AND GET DOWN!"* Nya of course was out of her mind with fear and screamed back, *"DON'T SHOOT ME! I'M A GOOD PERSON! I DIDN'T DO ANYTHING!"* One of the officer's screamed back, "I'm not going to shoot you, but get over there... **now!"**

Grandma started praying out loud, which brought a response of, "can you be quiet?" from one of the officers.

Grandma wanted to call somebody from her prayer group, which didn't go over too well.

"You can't call anybody; sorry," one of them told her. He grabbed her and, for some reason, attempted to gain access to her phone, but grandma had facial recognition and fingerprint identification as security features. After a few frustrating attempts at trying to get into grandma's phone, he threw it down on a chair in frustration.

One of the officers then asked us kids to please leave the room so that they could talk with grandma. They literally pushed us out; we left and went into the living room and sat on the couch with my aunt.

Back in grandma's bedroom, they informed her that they were, at that very moment, searching the house, looking for firearms and drugs. Now, usually in such situations, the police would force their way into a home or apartment and give the occupant (in this case, my grandma) the court-ordered search warrant at the front door. This basically allows the police free access to your home and and access to all of your belongings.

Well, that didn't quite happen here. I later found the search warrant **outside** of grandma's front door in the apartment complex hallway. At NO TIME during this whole episode did ANY of them present it to grandma; they just beat down the door, forced their way in and pretty much made themselves at home, doing and going through whatever they felt like.

They of course... found nothing in grandma's house. After about an hour, they finally left, empty-handed, and didn't even apologize for the mess or the inconvenience. I guess that would have been too much to ask.

****

After cleaning up the mess that the cops left behind in grandma's house, we called somebody from the city council and gave them the rundown as to what had just transpired. The city council passed the case on to the Delaware secretary of state's office, and they emailed us back a short time later, as did the woman from the city council *(we'll call her Mary)*.

The secretary of state's email said, in a nutshell, that the Wilmington police denied any and all involvement in what happened at grandma's that morning, but rather the state police and the FBI were the ones that had burst their way into the apartment. Now, NOWHERE in the email was there any reference to or explanation for why they burst into grandma's apartment: nothing.

Here's something worth pointing out: As I mentioned a few paragraphs back, I found the warrant outside grandma's apartment door in the hallway after everything had calmed down and law enforcement took off. Once again, it was never served to me when they came crashing into the apartment, which is legal protocol.

And right there, on the warrant itself, it mentioned that the attending law enforcement parties were the FBI, the state police and... that's right... the Wilmington PD.

Grandma immediately scanned that search warrant back to the secretary of state's office, but so far, we've heard nothing back from them. She sent a second email to see if the first email was received; again, no response.

So, with apparently nowhere else to turn, we re-attempted communication with Mary at the city council's office. Grandma sent her a small handful of emails and, not surprising, no response.

Now, here's what I have to assume about all of this: nobody cares. Period. The secretary of state's office, Mary at the city council... nobody. And why, you ask? I think you can read between the lines: it's because we're black, and we've been dealing with an incredibly racist police department that seems to take great delight in harassing us for reasons that just don't exist.

****

CONCLUSION

I'm finishing up this book during the last weeks of April, 2022. To date, nobody mentioned above has contacted grandma back at all, no phone calls, no emails, carrier pigeons, Pony Express riders, Western Union telegrams... nothing. The front door on grandma's house that was smashed up during law enforcement's last "visit" to her apartment has been fixed... sort of. The door itself requires three hinges, but the landlord only put... one... on the door, in the middle.

Not terribly safe against would-be burglars or fires.

And here's the BEST PART of all. A Fire Marshall inspector came by the building to check out another issue (he was already supposed to drop by grandma's apartment to see whether her new door met fire code standards). The inspector took a look at the replaced door (which is wooden, by the way, and not a metal safety door as is required by law) and the one hinge holding it up and said that everything... looked fine to him.

That's right. An exterior door that's meant to protect the apartment's inhabitants from the outside world and the threat of fire danger is being held up by one, single, solitary, hinge.

I guess they must have revised the city's fire code safety standards sometime during the night. Or maybe it's just... grandma's neighborhood that's getting the short end of the stick.

All of the teachers mentioned above are still employed at their respective schools and apparently have faced no legal action of any kind. And I'll bet you dollars to donuts that this will stay the same.

Going to school is still a bit of a nightmare for me. The teasing has pretty much subsided, but I still overhear a few snide comments here and there. But I'm at the point right now where I just don't care anymore. I used to go into the school bathroom and cry, thinking that it was all my fault, thinking that I somehow deserved this kind of treatment.

I remember my dad telling me the old sticks-and-stones adage, but I told him that the words DO hurt me. He told me something that I'll always carry with me: you're a beautiful, intelligent girl, stop looking down on yourself and, yes, your education is the most important thing here, not what a bunch of stupid classmates say.

Looking back at all this, it's safe to say that I learned a lifetime in a short time. I'll carry the physical and emotional scars with me for the rest of my days, but all of them have made me a stronger, better, more compassionate, tougher young woman. And if I ever have a daughter or a son of my own, I'll be sure to have him or her read this book when they're old enough to understand it.

The take-away? I'm my own best friend. I can count on one hand with a few fingers left over the number of people in this life that I can honestly trust. I'll never, EVER, let anyone push me around, physically or emotionally. I will NEVER treat anyone the way that I've been treated. I will get to know people better before I let them into my heart.

And I will carry with me the unfortunate notion that racism is still very much alive and well and living in Wilmington, if not the entire state of Delaware... not to mention the rest of America. Because if that same fire safety inspector had gone to a different apartment complex in another more upscale neighborhood, one with a different skin complexion, he would have had that door changed immediately, if not sooner. And had a white teenager been accused of stealing a cellphone, I'm sure that one, maybe two, police officers would have simply knocked on his or her parent's door and calmly discussed the situation at hand. No battering ram... no seven officers barging in, FBI agents, search warrants. No such nonsense.

Had a white teacher thrown a white student into a wall and bruised her entire body, it would have been all over the local news that same night. Legal investigations would kick into gear, lawyers, court hearings, lawsuits, victories for the white families involved, a disgraceful firing for the teacher involved... but so much for 'would-have' and 'should-have.'

Granted, that teacher was terminated. A bit of retribution is better than nothing.

The lessons I've learned from own betrayals will help and guide me through life. They're as much a part of me as my skin. But the betrayals foisted upon me and the rest of my family by those in positions of authority, such as teachers and school officials and state officials and city officials and law enforcement officers... that's a whole different ballgame.

And in this game, if you're black, the betrayals come hard and fast, each and every day. In my city and just about everywhere else.

Some things just never change. Is there hope in sight?

Not as far as I can see.

THE END...?